31 PRAYERS FOR MY SON

Aaron & Jennifer Smith

31 PRAYERS FOR MY SON
SON
Seeking God's Perfect Will for Him

Written By Aaron & Jennifer Smith
Cover By Ciera Rose - Cierarose.com
Interior Format & Layout By Miles Albritton

Copyright © 2017 Smith Family Resources, Inc.

ISBN-10: 0-9863667-2-2

ISBN-13: 978-0-9863667-2-7

LCCN: 2017916503

31prayersformyson.com

Printed in U.S.A

CONTENTS

CRY OUT IN THE NIGHT

"Arise, cry out in the night,
at the beginning of the night watches!
Pour out your heart like water
before the presence of the Lord!
Lift your hands to him
for the lives of your children"

Lamentations 2:19

INTRODUCTION

An olive tree is strong and sturdy. An olive tree is evergreen and always growing. It's a long lasting tree, some of which are well over 2,500 years old and still bearing fruit. An olive tree produces a bountiful blessing of rich and multifaceted fruit. It's wonderful contribution and significance has been a powerful reminder of God's ingenious design and generous provision from generation to generation. This tree is a true gift.

Likewise, your son is a true gift from God. Your son was thoughtfully and uniquely made by God. His character is developing as he matures into the man God created him to be. Like a solid tree, your son will be ever strong, masculine, and full of integrity. He is your son and it's good to celebrate who he is, who God is raising him up to be.

You were used by God to plant a seed, and that seed is your son. You are responsible for taking care of him as he grows, meeting his needs, watering him with the Word, praying for him and with him, and loving him unconditionally. You are the most significant and essential part of your son's life in leading him to Jesus.

"Train up a child in the way he should go; even when he is old he will not depart from it." Proverbs 22:6

Becoming a parent is truly a miraculous and incomparable experience. Being able to look into your child's eyes and immediately know, without a doubt, you have significant purpose in their life, is unparalleled and pure. God, in His infinite wisdom, created and established "family" to be a necessary and vital component for every society.

Life is precious to God, and in His goodness, He has entrusted you to protect life, to cultivate love in your family, so that life can thrive and the legacy of godliness and love can be passed down to the next generations.

Children are, and children will always be an extraordinary gift and blessing.

Your perspective and your heart toward children should resemble that of Christ...and He exemplified a heart for children.

"Then children were brought to him that he might lay his hands on them and pray. The disciples rebuked the people, but Jesus said, "Let the little children come to me and do not hinder them, for to such belongs the kingdom of heaven." And he laid his hands on them and went away." Matthew 19:13-14

You have been entrusted by God to raise up your son. Not only is it a huge blessing for you to be a significant part of his life, but in addition to that, you are doing an important work in his life. You are influencing him and training him up to be the man God has created him to be. You have the privilege of discipling his heart, teaching him God's ways, and setting the foundation for his future, every single day you get to spend with him. This work happens with every choice you make. Being a parent will seldom be easy or convenient, but it is worth it.

When you experience rough days, remember that your spouse and your children are not the enemy. You do have a real enemy and he is trying as hard as he can to destroy your family and devour your children. You must be prepared to fight for your family. You must be willing to enter into the battlefield, which is prayer.

Prayer is crucial. You must be willing to pray for your son every day. As you pray for your son, you will consider his greatest needs, seeking God's perfect will for him, petitioning God to provide for him and help him. Prayer is an awesome way to offer thanksgiving to God for your son and it is also a powerful way to defend against the enemy. As you faithfully purpose to pray for your son, you will inevitably experience intimacy with God. How awesome it is to know that by praying for your son, you are embracing a relationship with God and pursuing intimacy with Him!

My wife and I can personally testify to the power of prayer.

In the beginning of our marriage, when our relationship was falling apart, God reminded me every day not to give up praying for my wife. After 3.5 years of pain and turmoil, God heard our prayers and walked us through total transformation. This is why we agree with the Bible

and strongly encourage others to have a heart dedicated to prayer.

"Rejoice always, pray without ceasing, give thanks in all circumstances; for this is the will of God in Christ Jesus for you." 1 Thessalonians 5:16-18

Through our online ministries for husbands and wives (Husband Revolution & Unveiled Wife) we have heard some people admit they want to pray, but don't know how to pray. Hearing these stories moved us to write Thirty-One Prayers For My Wife and Thirty-One Prayers For My Husband. The feedback we have received from couples taking our 31 Prayer Challenge has been astounding. Testimonies continue to flood in from husbands and wives about how God is moving in their hearts and marriages.

We praise God for the breakthroughs marriages are experiencing because of these resources.

My wife and I also desire to be amazing parents. In our insecurities about parenting, being bombarded by fears and doubts, we call out to God and rely on Him and His Word to guide us in raising our children. God has been faithful to help us and walk with us through our parenting journey. We wrote this book because we want to help you and motivate you to pray for your son, or sons. Most of all we want you to draw closer to God through a life of prayer!

This resource is not a magical book that will solve your parenting questions, nor will praying these prayers guarantee
that you will have a perfect child. However, the Bible is clear

that we are to come to God and submit everything to Him in prayer.

"Do not be anxious about anything, but in everything by prayer and supplication with thanksgiving let your requests be made known to God." Philippians 4:6

Praying for your son's life will remind your heart not to worry, but rather trust in God and in His timing for everything.

This book is created to be an inspiration and launching point for you to continue to pray for your child. Our hope is that this will be a catalyst for you to pray every day of your child's life and give you creative ideas for things to pray for.

As you submit your heart to God in prayer, you will see Him move! It will be a wonderful day to hear a testimony from your son about how your prayers helped him! You can read these prayers straight from the text, you can say them out loud, you can get on your knees, or stand with your hands raised up toward the sky.

Please understand that we wrote this book in such a way that it is relevant for every son, regardless of age. These prayers could easily be for a 3 month old, as they could be for a 3 year old, even as they could be for a 13 year old. If there is a prayer that doesn't quite cover exactly what you are experiencing with your son we encourage you to make the prayer more personal by adding to it using the journal lines provided.

Remember he is God's son and God is going to be blessed

knowing you care so much for him that you are willing to make the time to pray for his life!

**We have included a few challenges to encourage you to consider the significance and purpose of praying for your children. There is a total of 7 challenges. We urge you to pray about each one and then fulfill it as the Lord leads you.

***We would also love to see your journey along the way! Update your social media and tag @unveiledwife and @husbandrevolution #PrayersForMySon so we can follow along and see how God is moving in your life, as well as in the lives of your children!

Our Prayer For You

Dear Heavenly Father,

Thank You for the parent reading this book. Thank You for the gift and blessing of their child. May You bless this family in great, big, beautiful ways. May Your Holy Spirit lead this family ever closer to You. May these prayers be used as a guide to bless, encourage, and anoint their awesome son as they petition for his heart and pray that one day he receives Your gift of salvation. May these prayers be used to bring this family closer to You, closer together, stronger, and more full of love than ever before.

In Jesus' name, AMEN!

A PRAYER FOR THE PARENT

Praying for your son is honorable. Throughout this book you will be praying for specific parts of his life and his future. As much as this is a huge initiative and selfless way of loving him, please don't skip over the importance of praying for your own heart and journey as his parent. Please devote time to praying and asking God to help you be the parent He created and desires you to be. This prayer is for you. Pray it as many times as you desire and add to it the areas of parenting you desire more wisdom and help from your Heavenly Father. He is faithful to encourage and equip you. Pray and listen. Then walk it out!

Dear Heavenly Father,

Thank You for entrusting me with my son. Thank You for the relationship we share. Thank You for the gift of becoming a parent. I pray my relationship with You serves to be a powerful example for my son. I pray You would continue to train me up to know You and know Your Word. Please send people into my life that have parenting experience, who also live according to Your Word. I pray they would lead me in my parenting and help me grow in the areas where I am weak. I pray You would mature my character, so that it reflects Your Holy character. I pray You would anoint my words and my actions toward my son. Help me to be compassionate toward him, especially when he is have a particularly hard day. I pray my son would always feel comfortable and safe talking with me. Help us to build trust with each other. I pray I would be quick to listen and slow to become angry. I pray I would respect him as the man you are raising him up to be. I pray I would be quick to apologize when I sin against him and that You would reconcile us if there is ever any conflict between us. I pray You would inspire me with creative ways to spend quality time with my son. Most of all, may You be glorified in our relationship.

In Jesus' name, AMEN!

DAY 1

A BLESSING FOR HIM

Psalm 127:3-5

DEAR LORD,

Thank You for the gift of my precious son. Thank You for creating him in Your image. Thank You for intentionally designing him with great purpose. I pray You would bless my son. I pray You would pierce my son's heart in a mighty way, that he would surrender his life to You. Reveal great and mighty things to him. Bless him with dreams about You and Your Kingdom. I pray You would bless my son with confidence in You. I pray You would raise him up to lead well, with all humility, in submission to You. I pray he would never doubt Your love for him. May he understand Your Word and may he rightly divide it. I pray Your Holy Spirit would guide my son throughout his life, protecting him from the snare of the enemy. I pray against the enemy's advances to destroy my son. Cover my son and uphold him with Your righteous right hand. May his life glorify You. I pray my son strives for righteousness. Bless my son with a heart of courage, that he may stand for truth. Bless him with strength. Bless him with the understanding of Your testimony and how to share it with others. I pray you would bless my son with good friends who deeply care for him. Bless my son with a wife who respects him. Bless him with children he can love, teach, and raise to know You. Bless my son in whatever job he has and bless him with the wisdom to steward all that You give to him. Bless my son with Your peace.

In Jesus' name, AMEN!

PERSONALIZE

Use this area to write a personalized prayer for your Son. You can also write a list of things you would like to continue to pray for.

CHALLENGE

- #1 -

START A PRAYER JOURNAL

Start a prayer journal that you will one day gift
to your child when he is older. Use this journal
to write down your prayers, specifically for your
son. Give it to him as a gift for a milestone
celebration such as his baptism, his graduation,
his wedding, or when he becomes a father.

DAY 2
SALVATION

Romans 10:9-10

DEAR LORD,

Thank You for Your steadfast love. Thank You for Your amazing gift of grace. Thank You for sending Your Son, Jesus Christ, to save us from our sin, that we may spend eternity with You. I pray I can be a light in my son's life, a pillar of truth, and I pray I teach him Your ways. I pray my son receives Your gift of Salvation. I pray You would anoint him with understanding and give him wisdom. I pray my son would believe in his heart that Jesus Christ died on a cross and that You raised Him from the dead. I pray my son would repent of his sin and turn from any wicked ways. I pray my son would confess with his mouth that Jesus is Lord and Savior. May he strive to live a righteous life. Soften the soil of my son's heart so that Your truth falls on rich ground. I pray Your Word would sprout in his heart and bear good fruit. Reveal Yourself to him in awesome ways. I pray my son remains faithful and steadfast. I pray my son would be an ambassador of Your light, sharing Your testimony boldly with all he meets. I pray there is no darkness in him at all. I pray there are no shadows in his heart. May Your light shine brightly through him, transforming him into the God-fearing man You desire him to be. I pray he looks forward to eternity with You. May he live a life that honors You.

In Jesus' name, AMEN!

PERSONALIZE

Use this area to write a personalized prayer for your Son. You can also write a list of things you would like to continue to pray for.

DAY 3

PURITY

Psalm 119:9

DEAR LORD,

Thank You for my son. Thank You for the personality he has. Thank You for the gifts and talents You have blessed him with. I love my son and I love getting to know him. I pray our relationship continues to grow. Help me to slow down, to meet him where he is at, and to be present in his life. Help me to be an intentional and good listener. I pray my son trusts me and confides in me for life's toughest challenges. I specifically ask that You would help my son to stay pure. Holy Spirit, please give my son a strong conviction to keep his ways pure. I pray he would divert his eyes when someone is dressed immodestly or when he passes by an explicit billboard. Give my son self-control when sensual ads pop-up online. I pray against the enemy and his ways to destroy my son's purity. Please guard my son from the enemy. I pray my son would apply the wisdom You give him and make choices that would preserve his purity. Help my son to understand that purity is power. I pray my son seeks purity in every aspect of his life including the music he listens to, the movies he watches, the books he reads, the websites he visits, and every other form of entertainment he exposes himself to. I pray he is pure in speech and pure in heart. May my son know Your Word so well that it guides him to know what is pure and how to keep his purity.

In Jesus' name, AMEN!

DAY 4
MADE IN GOD'S IMAGE

Genesis 1:26-27

DEAR LORD,

You are so amazing. You created us in Your image with thoughtfulness, precision, and purpose. The culture is fighting against You and what You have created. They are instigating and fueling confusion, instead of glorifying You. I pray my son is never deceived into believing lies about who he is, or that he was created with flaws. Instead, I pray my son appreciates the thoughtfulness You poured into his design when You formed him. I pray my son understands and accepts that he is a male, created in Your image. Help him to embrace the truth that he is an image bearer. Give him wisdom and help him comprehend the purpose of his design. I pray he values the fact he was created in Your image. Reveal awesome similarities between You and him that will make him proud to have been made in your image. I pray he embraces the qualities of masculinity. Holy Spirit, use me to affirm my son and confirm his identity in You. With all of the different things in this world begging for my son's attention, I pray my son identifies with Jesus Christ, and that he believes that is enough. I pray his identity in Christ is the foundation for his own personal acceptance of who he is and his abilities. I pray my son is an encouragement for other young men. I pray he is a positive role model for the younger generation. I pray my son walks confidently in Your wonderful truth.

In Jesus' name, AMEN!

CHALLENGE

- #2 -

CONSIDER THIS

Consider the thoughtfulness God poured into creating your son and making him in His image. Think about his unique character and his vast abilities. Take time to thank God for him. Then take a moment to share with your son all of the incredible things you considered about him.

DAY 5
INTEGRITY

Proverbs 11:3

DEAR LORD,

I pray my son walks with integrity all the days of his life. I pray my son is constant and steadfast. I pray my son is the same person in secret that he is in public. May he never do something for the approval of man, rather help him to do everything to please You alone. I pray he never shows favoritism to others. I pray he treats everyone with respect. Lord, please convict my son when he is tempted to sin and lead him to take the righteous path. Fill him with wisdom and help him to apply that wisdom. I pray my son has integrity in every area of his life and with all of his relationships. I pray he has integrity in the sports he plays, in the school work he completes, and in the jobs he has been assigned to. I pray my son has the quality of being honest. I pray he is a truth teller. May my son have strong moral principles established by Your Word. I also pray my son is not easily divided. Give him the capacity to fully give his attention when requested. I specifically pray for his relationship with his future wife and ask that You would help my son fully engage in conversation with her, listening and hearing, valuing her desire to be close to him. I also pray for his future as a father and ask that You help him have integrity in his parenting. May my son always search Your Word to guide him in his relationships. Help him navigate Your Word for prescription of how he should live his life. I pray my son has integrity when it comes to the way he manages money. I pray my son is a faithful man and a man of his word. I pray he is trustworthy and that others have an easy time believing and trusting him. I pray integrity would be a quality others see clearly in my son. I pray my son would be honored by all.

In Jesus' name, AMEN!

DAY 6

WISDOM

James 3:17

DEAR LORD,

Thank You for my son. Thank You for his heart and thank You for helping me teach him Your ways. I pray You would continue to use me in my son's life to bless him, teach him, and comfort him when he needs it. I pray I would be a good example of what it looks like to follow You. I pray I operate in wisdom every day. I also pray I can be someone who extends wisdom to my son. Help me to teach him diligently what I know. Thank You, Lord, for the gift of wisdom. You give it so generously. I pray for more wisdom. I ask You to fill my son full of wisdom. I pray he knows the difference between right and wrong. Help him to know how to apply the information he receives to live a healthy and righteous life. I pray he always chooses what is right. I pray my son would never try to justify terrible choices or sinful choices. I pray he would surround himself with wise friends. I pray he keeps people close to him who also choose to live righteous lives. I pray You would motivate my son to pursue wisdom. Give him a desire to acquire more knowledge. Show him how to do research and how to analyze data. I pray he is a quick learner. I pray he is someone others look to for advice and encouragement. I pray he humbly asks You for more wisdom. I pray against pride and I pray against a know-it-all attitude. May my son walk in humility, being slow to speak and slow to anger. Use my son and the wisdom You have given to him to turn hearts toward You.

In Jesus' name, AMEN!

BEING A PARENT

Being a parent is never convenient and your flesh will fight it. Yet, it is one of the most worthy things you will ever experience. Die to your flesh daily. Walk in the Spirit.

DAY 7
HARDWORKING

Proverbs 13:4

DEAR LORD,

You say in Your Word the soul of the diligent is richly supplied. I pray my son is diligent. I pray he is hardworking in everything he aims to do. Whether he is doing work at home around the house, working at a paid job, or lending a helping hand, I pray he works diligently. As he works, I pray that he shows care for the details of each task he completes. I pray he would be motivated to get his work done quickly, yet slow in his thoughtfulness and concern so that he never overlooks any part of what he is doing. I pray my son is thorough and always seeks to finish what he starts. I pray You would bless my son with endurance, especially when he has committed to difficult work days. Send others to encourage him and affirm him in the job he is doing. Help me to encourage him as well. I also pray You would use me as an example to my son of what it looks like to be diligent. I pray I would not be lazy and that I would have a good attitude when it comes to work that needs to be done. I pray my son never struggles with being lazy. Holy Spirit, please help him to have a good attitude, a joyful attitude, no matter what the magnitude of the job is. I pray my son grows into becoming a man who accepts hard jobs with gratitude. I pray he is hardworking and willing to do whatever it takes to be a provider for his family. Please give my son ingenuity and creativity as he focuses on doing his work diligently.

In Jesus' name, AMEN!

DAY 8
A SERVANT HEART

Acts 20:35

DEAR LORD,

Thank You for sending Jesus Christ, who is the perfect example of how to live righteously. I pray my son would study Jesus and become familiar with all of His ways. I pray my son would desire to have a servant heart just like Jesus. Holy Spirit, transform my son and mold him to be a man after Your own heart. I pray my son is full of compassion. I pray he seeks the interests of others above himself. When selfishness rises up in his heart, I pray he recognizes it and asks You to change him. I pray his eyes are aware of others who are in need and I pray he is quick to help them. I pray my son believes it is more blessed to give than to receive. I pray this is a truth he experiences first hand. When my son does give generously, may You bless him with joy. Satisfy his heart. May he feel fulfilled in the purpose You created him for. I pray he lifts up those who are weak, using Your Word to encourage them. I pray he is a constant comfort for those closest to him. When I ask him for help, I pray he is quick to take action without complaining. I pray against a poor attitude. I pray against laziness. I pray my son would do everything with a pure heart, knowing that he is serving You. May he never do anything out of selfish ambition or vain conceit. Let love motivate his heart. I pray my son is eager to be a helper. I pray You anoint him with strength and endurance so that he is capable of doing difficult tasks. I pray that in everything he gives You the glory.

In Jesus' name, AMEN!

CHALLENGE

- #3 -

WRITE GOD A LETTER

Share with Him your whole heart, your hopes and fears about parenting, and what you are currently feeling or experiencing.

DAY 9

CONTENTMENT

Philippians 4:11-13

DEAR LORD,

No matter what circumstances my son faces in his lifetime, I pray he learns how to remain content. Whether with much or with little, I pray my son gives You thanks for it all. May his heart be truly grateful for all that You provide. May he have an appreciation for the gift of life that satisfies him completely. May he understand that what You do provide is a gift. I pray my son never grumbles or complains because of his circumstances. I also pray his circumstances are not a catalyst for his attitude to shift toward the negative. May my son know how to exercise self-control and respond in difficult times with steadfastness. I pray he would have a right perspective, Your perspective. Give him eyes to see the world as You see it. May his heart remain humble. I pray he never entertains the thought that You owe him what his heart desires. I pray he would lay his desires at the foot of Your throne and accept what You have for him with true appreciation. I pray his contentment would be a light in this dark world. I pray others would recognize his contentment and inquire about it so that my son can give them an answer that points their hearts toward You. I pray I also am a content person, one who responds to circumstances with perseverance and trust in You. Thank You for all of the wonderful gifts You do provide every single day. Thank You for Your goodness.

In Jesus' name, AMEN!

DAY 10
HIS EDUCATION
Proverbs 18:15

DEAR LORD,

Thank You for the gift of learning. You have given us incredible access to all kinds of information. You have even made Your Word abundantly accessible. I pray my son would desire to gain more understanding and more knowledge. May he absorb information like a sponge. Help him to retain what he learns. I pray my son would value his education. Please anoint him with great comprehension and the ability to learn quickly. Bless him with fine skill as he acquires more and more through education. If it be in Your will that my son attends a vocational school or college, I pray he would diligently pursue his certificate of completion. I pray he is able to excel while remaining debt free. Please provide for him whatever means necessary to keep learning. I pray he uses his knowledge to do good in this world. I pray my son would use his education to further Your Kingdom. I pray You would continue to build his tool belt through education and experience. Regardless of his age, may he always be motivated to gain more knowledge. I pray as my son continues to learn that he would acquire a heart of discernment. I pray he would be able to judge well. I pray he tests all of the information he receives according to Your Word. If anything is contradictory to Your Word, may he be quick to stand firmly in Your truth, unwavering by the world's ideology. Lead my son and may he obey You with reverence. Thank You, Lord, for maturing my son through the gift of education. I pray he is always willing to bless others with his knowledge, to teach with passion and kindness, to see the potential in others and affirm them.

In Jesus' name, AMEN!

DAY 11
PURSUING GOD

Deuteronomy 4:29

DEAR LORD,

I pray my son never stops pursuing You. I pray my son seeks to read Your Word and pray every day. May he have a desire to know You more intimately. I pray my son is open and honest with You, willing to share with You everything. I pray he shares with You the deepest places in his heart. Help him not to be afraid of being known by You. I pray You would drag his sin into the light and expose it for what it is. I pray my son would cast off anything that easily entangles him. I pray against the temptation to sin. Strengthen my son in those moments and help him escape. I pray my son would run to You and trust You for strength to overcome. May he walk in victory all the days of his life. I pray against sexual addiction, drug addiction, food addiction, and any other vice that would try to keep him in bondage. Lord, may Your Holy Spirit lead him to walk in the freedom You have provided for him. I pray my son walks so closely to You that he would never be in a compromising situation. Keep him far from danger. I pray my son seeks You with all of his heart and that he finds You. Reveal Yourself to him in great and mighty ways. I pray my son recognizes all of the ways You are pursuing him. I pray he confidently knows how much he is loved by You. Take him on an incredible journey of getting to know You more. Thank You Lord, for Your gift of grace. You are awesome.

In Jesus' name, AMEN!

THE GREATEST EXAMPLE

The greatest example of love you can show your child is the way you love your spouse. Let your marriage be the reason he desires to get married one day.

DAY 12
COURAGE

Joshua 1:9

DEAR LORD,

I pray my son is courageous. I pray he would not wrestle with fear or insecurities. May You bless him with strength. I pray he experiences strength in the face of pain or grief. I pray he has the ability to defend the weak and be a protector for those in need. I pray the threat of evil never scares him to the point of paralysis. Help him to do what You need him to do regardless of what the enemy is doing. Keep his mind clear while in the midst of dangerous situations. Help him to respond with wisdom. Help him to stay calm. May he be bold, standing on the foundation of Your truth. I pray he would be confident knowing You are with him wherever he goes. I pray against the enemy's tactics that incite fear. I pray against anxious thoughts. May he be overwhelmed by Your peace. Lord, I ask that You would protect my son's mind. Guard his mind and his heart from evil. I pray he would boldly share Your Gospel with everyone. I pray he would never shrink back from doing the right thing. I pray my son becomes a man of courage. May he navigate all of his relationships with courage to say what needs to be said in truth and in love. I pray he is a man of bravery. I pray he relies on You to strengthen him.

In Jesus' name, AMEN!

DAY 13
HIS ATTITUDE

Philippians 2:14-16

DEAR LORD,

Thank You for my son. I pray for his attitude. I pray his mental state is one of clarity. I pray he has a right perspective of the world and of people. May he see with Your perspective. I pray his behavior reflects a righteous attitude. I pray as his behavior reflects the posture of his heart, that it would be evident he is a follower of You. I pray my son submits his attitude to You. I pray circumstances do not easily influence change in his attitude. Instead, I pray he is constant and steadfast, believing that You are his helper. When he is asked to do difficult tasks, may he do it without complaint. I pray his attitude reflects appreciation and gratefulness. I pray he is willing to do what is asked of him with joy. May his attitude be contagious, spreading joy to other people, being a catalyst to change their attitudes into ones that reflect joy. I pray my son would be found pure and blameless in Your eyes. I pray my son would never have a negative attitude against You. I pray he would never wrestle with being angry at You. If he is tempted to have a poor attitude toward You, toward his family, or toward anyone, please convict his heart and transform him. Remove the root cause of any bad attitude that rises up, so that it does not grow wildly out of control. I pray my son would be aware of how his facial expressions and body language reveal his attitude. I pray he operates with self-control at all times. I pray my son is gracious in the way he expresses himself.

In Jesus' name, AMEN!

CHALLENGE

- #4 -

WRITE A RESPONSE

Write a response to your letter to God, from God's perspective. What do you think He would say to encourage you?

DAY 14
A PROTECTOR

Psalm 138:7

DEAR LORD,

Thank You for being our protector. Thank You for being our Savior. I lift up my son and ask that he acknowledges You as his protector. I pray he trusts in You to protect him. I pray he has a personal and deep appreciation for Jesus Christ going to the cross to save him. I pray You would preserve his life. If my son is ever in the midst of trouble, please reach out Your hand and save him. Lift him up out of trouble and secure him. I pray my son would have a humble heart and be thankful for the ways You have been there for him and will continue to be there for him. I also pray my son is a protector. I pray he seeks to protect his own heart from danger. May he be filled with wisdom and may he apply it every day. I pray my son protects his purity. I pray my son protects his mind from the filthy ways of this world. I pray he is a protector of others as well. Give him eyes to see when trouble is happening to others and give him courage to step in and rescue whoever is in danger. Protect him as he boldly defends the weak. I pray he would be a man who protects his family. Thank You for raising my son up to be a protector. I pray others are blessed by his courage in the face of evil. I pray his bravery and strength are a testament of Your power. If any evil comes against my son, I pray You would protect him from it. If anyone speaks evil of him or slanders his reputation, please protect him. May you preserve his life so that through him Your name and Your good news is spread over the earth.

In Jesus' name, AMEN!

DAY 15
FRUIT OF THE SPIRIT

Galatians 5:22-23

DEAR LORD,

Thank You for the fruit of the Spirit. Thank You for producing this fruit in the lives of those who abide in You. I pray my son abides in You. I pray this fruit is abundant in his life. I pray my son loves all people with great love. I pray he is full of peace and that he is a peacemaker. I pray my son is patient in all of his ways. May kindness be an attribute that others admire and appreciate in him. I pray he is good and sees good in others. May he be a man of faithfulness, faithful to You and faithful to his family. May he be gentle, especially to women and children. I pray my son exercises self-control in every area of his life. Holy Spirit, please continue to mature my son. Feed and water his heart with Your truth, that he may have even more fruit produced in him. I pray others would taste and see that You are good because of him. I pray others benefit because of his faith in You. Thank You for the fruit of the Spirit. I pray You would prune any sin in my son's life. Prune any dead areas of his heart that bear no fruit. Prune anything that leads to death. I pray he comes to undertsand that pruning is a necessary process that refines him and results in more fruit being produced. As a gardener nurtures his garden, may You nurture my son's heart and character. Use me to also help him grow up in You. Thank You for my son! Thank You for the gift he is to me and to everyone else who is a part of his life.

In Jesus' name, AMEN!

DAY 16

HIS PURPOSE

Proverbs 19:21

DEAR LORD,

Thank You for creating my son with purpose. I pray my son believes he has great purpose. I pray he lives a life dedicated to fulfilling his purpose. Give him the ability to discern what his purpose is and how he can fulfill it. Any plans that he has, I pray he would surrender them to You and allow You to lead him. Stir up extraordinary plans in his heart. Inspire him to think outside of the box. Give him creativity and passion as he seeks to fulfill Your will for his life. I pray my son finds purpose even in the simple things. I pray he finds purpose in being kind, in being a good friend, in taking care of his family. I pray he finds purpose in his job. I pray he finds purpose in being a positive role model and an honorable citizen. Show him why he is valuable. I pray my son never believes the lies from the enemy that his life means nothing. Help him never to doubt that he is wanted and loved. I pray he always knows that his life matters. I pray he takes care of himself and has a deep appreciation for life. I pray Your purpose for my son prevails. Use me to affirm my son and to encourage him. Use me to bless him with resources to help him fulfill his purpose. Use me to comfort him and to remind him that he is of great worth. I pray my son seeks to please you every day. May he practice righteousness. I ask You to guide him and direct his every step. Uphold him with Your righteous right hand.

In Jesus' name, AMEN!

DAY 17
LOVE & ROMANCE

1 Corinthians 13:4-8

DEAR LORD,

Your love is transforming. Your love is powerful. Your love is a gift that continues to give. I pray my son is a person who loves with everything he's got. I pray he is patient and kind. I pray he is quick to listen and slow to speak. May he be a person who doesn't keep records of people's wrongs, but forgives with sincerity. I pray my son is tender hearted and gentle toward all men, women, and children. I pray he is gentle in his actions and words. Help him to have self-control in all of his actions and reactions. I pray he is not rude. I also pray he is not prideful. I pray he loves people and extends grace to them. I pray my son matures into a man who loves and cherishes his future wife. I pray he understands the value of romance and finds creative ways to show his wife his love for her. I pray he tells her he loves her every day. I pray she receives his love and confidently knows that You love her. I pray my son loves his family just as You love. Thank You for Your example of love and thank You for defining love in Your Holy Word. May my son be an advocate of Your good love. I pray he is hopeful, enduring all things and bearing with others in love. I pray he never fails at loving others. Thank You for the gift of Your love. I pray my son never doubts my love for him. I pray my love blesses him. May You be glorified as we seek to share Your love with others.

In Jesus' name, AMEN!

DISCIPLING THE HEART

You are responsible for discipling the heart of your child. Teach him God's ways by walking with integrity every single day.

DAY 18

PEACE

Philippians 4:7

DEAR LORD,

I pray my son seeks peace and pursues it. I pray he trusts in You to give him peace. When trials and tribulation come his way, may You secure his heart with Your peace. I pray my son is a peacemaker with all. When conflict arises, please help him navigate the treacherous waters of relationships, leading to peaceful reconciliation. Help him choose his words carefully, that with them he brings peace to all. I pray my son carries Your peace with him wherever he goes. I pray against the evil one and his evil schemes to steal my son's peace. I pray against the enemy trying to strike fear in my son. I pray against doubt and insecurity. I pray against worry and anxiety. I pray against the enemy trying to make my son stumble. I pray not one of his schemes come to pass. I pray my son finds peace in Your Word. I pray he reads Your Word to be filled with Your peace. I pray his feet remain secure. I pray his mind remains clear and confident in You. In any major decisions my son has to make, I pray he seeks Your peace on the matter. I pray he desires to please You. May Your presence bring peace to his heart and mind, reminding him that You are near. I pray there is peace in my relationship with my son. I pray we talk to each other kindly. I pray we encourage one another and provide comfort to each other. Thank You for the peace that You give. If my son is ever overcome with anxiety may You help him be still and trust in You. Bless my son with Your peace that surpasses all understanding.

In Jesus' name, AMEN!

DAY 19

PRAYER WARRIOR

1 Thessalonians 5:16-18

DEAR LORD,

Thank You for giving us access to communicate with You through prayer. I pray my son understands prayer. May he desire to pray every day. Use me to teach him how to pray. May he search Your Word for teachings on prayer and live accordingly. I pray my son is quick to respond to circumstances he faces with a humble heart of prayer. I pray he is a prayer warrior, fighting the good fight of faith. May he pray for himself, his family, and for others. May he pray against the enemy and his attacks. When he is tempted to sin, may he pray and ask You for help to escape that temptation. When he is trying to comfort someone, may he offer to pray with them. When obstacles get in his way or when trials pummel him, may he remain steadfast and pray. May he come to You with thankfulness for all that You have done. May he rejoice and bless Your name. I pray my son uses prayer to offer You his heart and to share all that he is experiencing, with faith that You will be his helper. May he boldly pray with his friends and his church fellowship. May he feel confident to pray in the presence of one or of many. I pray You would hear his prayers and respond. May my son pray continually. I pray he never gives up, rather may his faith in You increase. May answered prayers be affirmation in his relationship with You and a powerful testimony that encourages others. May prayer be an anchor in his life. I pray my son is obedient to You in praying without ceasing.

In Jesus' name, AMEN!

CHALLENGE

- #5 -

THE MOST IMPORTANT THING

Salvation is the most important thing. Spend time kneeling in prayer, petitioning on behalf of your son, praying that he accepts Jesus Christ as his personal Lord and Savior and that he spends his life seeking after God wholeheartedly.

DAY 10

HIS MIND

Romans 12:2

DEAR LORD,

I pray for my son's mind. I pray You would protect my son's mind. I pray he would not be overwhelmed with negative thoughts. I also pray he would not suffer from nightmares. Guard his mind in Christ. I pray he would not believe lies, but instead test everything according to Your truth. Please protect his mind from lustful temptation. Teach him how to have self-control of his thoughts. I pray he submits his thoughts to You. I pray his thoughts are pure. I pray he does not dwell on negative thoughts about people or circumstances. May my son be able to recognize the positive and give thanks to You always. I also pray his mind works at high efficiency. I ask that You keep his mind sharp and sober. I pray my son thinks clearly and can focus without distractions. I pray he never battles with insecurity or self-doubt. I pray he never suffers from having a skewed perception of himself or others. Please give him peace of mind. As Your relationship with my son grows, I pray You would transform him by the renewing of his mind. May he be like-minded with You. I pray my son wouldn't conform to the ways of this world. I pray he would test everything according to Your Word. I pray he would become a man of logic and reason, with a strong foundation built on truth. I pray his faith continues to increase. When evil or negative thoughts come into his mind, please remove them right away.

In Jesus' name, AMEN!

DAY 21

SELF-CONTROL

Proverbs 25:28

DEAR LORD,

Thank You for my son. He is a blessing to me. Thank You for who You created him to be. I love You. I lift up my son to You. I pray my son exercises self-control every day. I pray he has self-control in his emotions, his thoughts, his actions, his speech, his diet, and in everything. May he be anointed with Your strength to have restraint when it comes to these areas of life. I pray my son's ability to have self-control protects him from experiencing brokenness and pain in his life. I pray his ability to have self-control keeps him out of dangerous situations. Please build up in him a habit of self-control. I pray I would be a positive example for my son of what it looks like to exercise self-control. Holy Spirit, convict my heart when I operate without self-control so that I may repent and be transformed. I desire my son to know the importance of being a person who has self-control. As my son experiences a wide variety of emotions, may he be able to process those emotions without reacting inappropriately. I pray my son would not allow anger or rage to motivate him to respond violently. Help him to identify his emotions and to work through them with restraint. I also pray my son is able to express himself vulnerably. I pray he doesn't hold back sensitive emotions such as crying because he thinks he needs to be strong. Give him understanding with his emotions. I pray his heart is sensitive to Your leading. Point out to him any areas of his life where he needs to have more self-control. May he be transformed by You, Lord.

In Jesus' name, AMEN!

DAY 11

HIS HEALTH

1 Corinthians 6:19-20

DEAR LORD,

Thank You for my son. I pray You would bless my son with good health. Make him strong and able to endure. I pray against any disease that would try to attack his body. I pray against any virus or bacteria that would threaten his immune system. I pray You would give my son an incredible immune system that always works great. Please protect his health. I pray my son is proactive about his health. May Your Holy Spirit remind him every day that his body is a temple for You and that he is responsible to care for it. Give him wisdom in how to care for his body. Teach him what types of food he should eat and how to make wise decisions about food. I pray he would not struggle with food addictions or use food to cope with difficult circumstances. I pray he would have self-control with eating, and rely on You to get him through tough times. I pray my son would exercise regularly and challenge his body to be active. I pray physical activity would not cause him pain. I pray against laziness. I pray my son would be health conscience, making decisions that will prolong his life. I pray he would be a protector for others by looking out for their health. Give him boldness to encourage others to live healthy lifestyles. I pray against the temptations of drugs, alcohol, or anything that could damage my son's body. Give him the strength and courage to say no to those temptations. Surround him with friends who also desire to live healthy lives, friends who will protect him from being tempted in that way. Help my son to rest often and to not let stress rule in his body.

In Jesus' name, AMEN!

DAY 23

HUNGRY FOR THE WORD

2 Timothy 3:16-17

DEAR LORD,

You have given us the amazing gift of Your Holy Word. Thank You for the Bible. Thank You for the scriptures that You have provided for us to live by as a manual. I pray my son always has access to the Bible. I pray he takes care of his Bible and treats it with care. I pray he values it as Holy. I pray he believes Your Word as truth and inerrant. I pray he uses Your Word for teaching and correction. I pray he uses the Bible to be trained in righteousness. May Your Holy Word equip my son for every good work that You have prepared for him to do. I pray my son is hungry for Your Word, that he may consume it every day. I pray Your Word guides him and directs his every step. When he is presented with information or an ideology the culture approves, may he test it according to Your Word and support only what is truth. Help my son to rightly divide Your Word, being obedient to all that You command. I pray he can stand on Your Word with boldness of faith. I pray he would know Your Word well. I pray he knows how to navigate Your Word so that he can direct others to it. I pray my son professes Your Holy Word with courage and teaches Your Word to others. May he be an ambassador of Your truth to this suffering world. I pray my son would always have a teachable heart, humble, and ready to learn Your Word. Write Your Word on the tablet of his heart.

In Jesus' name, AMEN!

DON'T LISTEN

Don't listen to the enemy when he tries to convince you that you are failing as a parent. Don't let insecurity or doubt invade your heart. Be confident in your relationship with God in Christ Jesus and know that He is moving through you for an extraordinary purpose.

DAY 24

STRENGTH

Ephesians 6:10

DEAR LORD,

I pray my son is filled with Your strength. I pray he asks You to strengthen him every day. I pray he intentionally puts on the full armor that You provide for him. I pray he is prepared for any spiritual battle that comes his way. I pray he trusts in You and relies on You to lead him through it all. Train him to call upon Your name, especially in times of trouble. I pray my son matures into a man of strength and power. I pray he grows into a man of stature that reveals his strength. I pray his posture and his heart both reflect the mental power and physical power he has. May You use his abilities for good. I pray his strength is used to bless others and protect others. I pray my son has vigor to do difficult tasks. I pray he is willing to challenge himself to use his strength in an honorable way. I pray my son gives You the glory for his strength. Make him strong to fight against the enemy. Make him strong to defend the weak. Make him strong so he can fight the good fight of faith. Make him strong to stand for his faith in this dark world. Make him strong to support his family. Make him strong to carry out Your will. Help my son to stand strong against the enemy's schemes. Prepare his heart and strengthen him every day for all that he will encounter. I pray my son would have endurance to persevere no matter what his circumstances are. May You be his source of life, of joy, of peace, and of strength.

In Jesus' name, AMEN!

DAY 25

HIS FRIENDS

Proverbs 13:20

DEAR LORD,

Thank You for my son. Thank You for the friends You have blessed him with. I pray my son can be a light into each one of their lives. I pray he would be a good friend, a trustworthy friend, and a friend that loves with a pure heart. I pray my son would encourage his friends to follow You. I pray he would remind them that they have a purpose and that they have gifts to bless others with. I pray my son would help support his friends as they strive to reach their potential. I pray his friends would do the same for him. I pray my son's friends would remind him daily to seek after God. I pray they would speak truth into his life and encourage him to experience the extraordinary. I pray my son's friends are good to him. I pray my son and his friends take advantage of opportunities to work together to fulfill Your will, to help others, and to contribute to the well being of their local community. I pray my son's friend's families know You. I pray they are supportive of their friendships. I pray they teach their sons to live with moral integrity. May these boys grow up to be husbands and fathers who lead according to Your Word. Bless these friendships, Lord. Unite them with a strong bond. Give them courage to build each other up. Give them wisdom to lead them as they go. May they be comrades in faith, encouraging each other to fulfill Your will.

In Jesus' name, AMEN!

DAY 26
LOVING FAMILY

John 13:34

DEAR LORD,

Thank You for my son. I pray he has a great love for his family. I pray he is always willing to be present with us. I pray he is intentional with spending time with us. I pray he is willing to participate in the activities that we desire him to do, such as family game nights. I pray he understands that our time with him is precious, because no one is guaranteed tomorrow. I pray our conversations go deep beneath the surface of our hearts. May he always be willing to be transparent with the things he is wrestling with internally, trusting that I am here to help him and comfort him through it. I pray You would help me be a good listener. Help me to love my son unconditionally. I pray against the distraction of technology getting in the way of close fellowship. Give my son a desire to be present that is stronger than his desire to be engaged with a phone, computer, or gaming system. I pray he is always there for his family, willing to encourage and help when needed. Give him creative ways to bless his family. Cultivate strong relationships between him and his family. I pray he would genuinely enjoy our company. When conflicts arise with family, please give my son wisdom in how to handle it appropriately and righteously. As my son grows up and experiences hormonal changes, please help him to respond to circumstances with self-control. I pray You would use me to help him navigate changes in his body so that he has understanding. I pray it is evident to all that our family is one that loves unconditionally.

In Jesus' name, AMEN!

CHALLENGE

- #6 -

PRAY WITH HIM

Cultivate a relationship with your son where prayer is a priority. Ask him how he is doing and offer to pray with him. You can even ask him to make a list for you as a guide to pray for his specific needs throughout the week.

DAY 27
YIELDED TO THE LORD

Proverbs 3:5-6

DEAR LORD,

Thank You for my son. I pray for a special opportunity to affirm my son today. Give me courage to speak words of encouragement into his life. I pray that in everything I do and say I respect my son. May we have a moment to embrace each other and love each other, regardless of what might be going on around us. I pray my son trusts in You. I pray he doesn't lean on his own understanding, but rather leans on You. I pray he would be yielded to You. I pray his heart is humble before You. I pray he allows You to lead him. I pray my son has an insatiable desire to read Your Word, knowing that Your Word will guide him. Direct his every step. Holy Spirit, speak to my son, convict his heart of any sin, and reconcile him to Yourself. I pray my son would be righteous in all of his ways. I pray he would not trust his own heart, but rather he would trust You completely. I pray I would be a good example to him of how to lean on You. I pray he would see that in the everyday moments that I seek You, as I read Your Word, as I pray, and as I worship You. I pray my son would also submit his plans to You and ask You to lead him through those plans. I pray he is more concerned with fulfilling Your will than his own will. I pray he also allows me to help lead him as he matures. Help him to see that his obedience to his parents will help him in his obedience to You.

In Jesus' name, AMEN!

DAY 18
HIS CHARACTER

2 Timothy 2:22-26

DEAR LORD,

Thank You for my son. I love getting to know him. I enjoy watching his personality develop. I love seeing You move in his life. I pray You would continue to refine my son's character. Mold him and make him to be more like You. I pray the way he thinks, the way he feels, and the way he behaves would be acceptable and pleasing to You. I pray my son would flee evil desires and pursue righteousness, faith, love, and peace. When he is tempted, please show him how to escape that temptation. I pray my son has nothing to do with foolishness. I pray he avoids ignorant controversies and quarrels. Help him to never gossip about others. I pray my son lives with moral convictions that make him a man worthy to be praised. Protect my son from the pain and consequences of other people's sin. I pray my son's character is holy as You are holy. I pray people who know my son are encouraged to also live a holy life. May his love for You draw others closer to You. I pray his character and moral convictions are a light in the world. I pray people wonder why he chooses to be holy and that my son would direct them toward You. May You be glorified through my son's character. I pray other boys and men are encouraged to have a godly character because of my son. I pray my son would have a pure heart. I pray he would be compassionate toward others. May my son mature to have a character just like You!

In Jesus' name, AMEN!

DAY 19
LIKE CHRIST

1 John 2:1-6

DEAR LORD,

I pray my son would be like Christ. I pray he would be loving, passionate, knowledgeable, and full of truth. I pray he would spend time with You every day. I pray he would be compassionate. I pray he would be willing to sacrifice anything in his life if that was Your will. May nothing ever get in the way of his love for You. I pray my son would walk as Jesus walked, with courage to speak the Gospel. I pray others would recognize Jesus when they look at my son. I pray my son would be a reflection of Your testimony. May he be a light in this dark world, guiding people to the foot of Your throne. I pray my son would not sin. If he does sin, I pray he repents of his wrong doing. Turn his heart to be forever toward You, Lord. I pray my son would abide in You and keep Your commands. I pray he would be obedient to Your Holy Word. As Your relationship with my son continues to grow, I pray he would know You intimately. I pray he would let You know who he is. I pray he would allow You to speak into his life and guide him. I pray You would bring other people into his life that walk as Jesus walked. May they encourage him in faith and in righteousness. I pray my son embraces community. I pray he walks humbly and vulnerably with other people. Use my son to encourage others. I pray my son would be Jesus' hands and feet, serving others joyfully. I pray he knows Your Word just as good as Jesus.

In Jesus' name, AMEN!

LOVE YOUR FAMILY

Love your family by taking time to sit with them today. Listen to them, play with them, read to them, teach them, pray with them. You are not guaranteed tomorrow...so don't forsake the opportunities you have today to be with them and share God's love with them.

DAY 30
AN EXTRAORDINARY LIFE

James 1:25

DEAR LORD,

Thank You for my son's life. Thank You for trusting me to be his parent. Thank You for giving us the time to bond and experience the awesome gift of our relationship. Thank You for the love he has for You and for others. Thank You for being there for him, protecting him, guiding him, and for maturing him. I pray my son lives an extraordinary life. I pray he intentionally pursues an extraordinary life. May Your Holy Spirit lead him to incredible opportunities that advance Your Kingdom. I pray my son is a warrior for You. I pray he is never afraid to take chances, having faith that You are with him. I pray he would have an abundance of wisdom to help him navigate where You want him to go and what You desire him to do. I pray my son believes You set him free from the bondage of sin, and that he uses his freedom to serve You. I pray he always remains a doer of Your Word. Help my son to see the extraordinary in everyday life. Whether he is on a nature walk and examines Your creation or is with a group of friends experiencing the gift of love, may he give You the glory for it all. I pray he has eyes to see the extraordinary gifts You have lavished him with. I pray my son and I have an incredible relationship. I pray You would give us opportunities to spend quality time together, to be present and to talk. I pray my son and I love each other deeply and pray for one another daily. I pray we both submit our lives to You in reverence and fear. You are our God!

In Jesus' name, AMEN!

DAY 31

AN EXTRAORDINARY MARRIAGE

Ephesians 5:22-33

DEAR LORD,

You are so amazing. You are good! Your love endures forever. Your faithfulness is never-ending. Thank You for Your provision. Thank You for Your gift of grace. I pray for my son and I lift up his future to You. I pray my son has a positive perspective of marriage and understands the purpose of marriage. I pray he understands why You created marriage and I pray he has a desire to be married. If it is in Your will for my son, I pray he experiences marriage. I pray for his future wife. Bless her, Lord. Prepare her heart for marriage. May Your Holy Spirit guide my son and his future wife as they navigate dating and then marriage. I pray his wife believes Jesus Christ is Lord and Savior, confessing it with her mouth. I pray her family knows You and believes in You as well. I pray my future daughter-in-law fears You and loves You with all of her heart. I pray she respects my son and loves him unconditionally. May they embrace being one in marriage, may they pursue intimacy, and may they serve You together as a team. I pray my son cherishes his wife and intentionally pursues her romantically. I pray their marriage is a reflection of Your love for all. Use their marriage to draw others closer to Yourself. I pray they pursue intimacy with You and work together to serve others joyfully. I pray they experience an extraordinary marriage.

In Jesus' name, AMEN!

CHALLENGE

- #7 -

HIS FUTURE

Marriage is a wonderful gift to look forward to. Invite your son to pray with you for his future wife.

PRAY FOR YOUR MARRIAGE

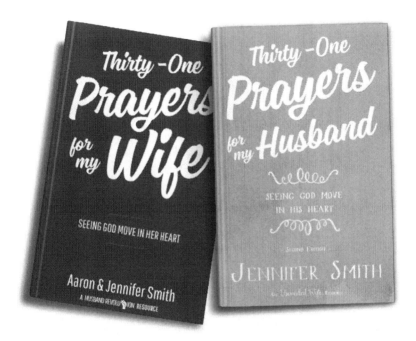

My wife and I wrote these two books to help inspire couples to pray for each other. Grab this bundle and take the 31-day challenge to pray for each other.

Visit Our Store Today
Shop.unveiledwife.com

GROW CLOSER TO GOD & EACH OTHER

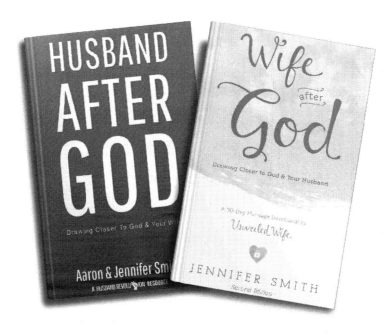

These two complementary resources walk through important biblical marriage principles, while also addressing different areas of life that a husband and wife might struggle with.

Visit Our Store Today
Shop.unveiledwife.com

GREAT GIFT IDEA FOR SINGLES & ENGAGED

These are great resources to help teenagers purpose their hearts for what God has for their future marriage or anyone else who feels strongly about getting married and cares for the heart of their future spouse.

Visit Our Store Today
Shop.unveiledwife.com

FRAMEABLE ART

Praying for your son is a beautiful way of loving him. Be reminded of the time you have spent praying for him and be reminded to continue praying for him with this detailed watercolor print of the olive tree from the cover of this book.

When we decided to make "The Olive Tree" print for you, we envisioned it hanging in your son's nursery or bedroom as a thoughtful reminder for him and for you that he is being prayed for!

5 x 7 or 8 x 10 full color prints available only at our online store:

Shop.unveiledwife.com/prints

If this prayer book has impacted your faith please let me know by posting a testimony here:
31prayersformydaughter.com

For more marriage resources please visit:
shop.unveiledwife.com

Sign-up for daily prayers by email:
unveiledwife.com/daily-prayer/
husbandrevolution.com/daily-prayer/

Get connected:
Facebook.com/unveiledwife
Instagram.com/unveiledwife

Facebook.com/husbandrevolution
Instagram.com/husbandrevolution

Made in the USA
Middletown, DE
16 June 2021